The Lincolns from A to Z

by

Betty Carlson Kay

authorHOUSE®

AuthorHouse™
1663 Liberty Drive, Suite 200
Bloomington, IN 47403
www.authorhouse.com
Phone: 1-800-839-8640

First published by AuthorHouse 2/29/2008

ISBN: 978-1-4343-6827-0 (sc)

Library of Congress Control Number: 2008901019

Printed in the United States of America
Bloomington, Indiana

This book is printed on acid-free paper.

*This book is dedicated to
the next generation
of Lincoln scholars*

All photographs used in this book are courtesy of the

**Abraham Lincoln Presidential
Library and Museum**

with special thanks to

Rick Beard, Director, ALPLM

Tom Schwartz, State Historian

Jennifer Ericson

Mary Michaels

Table of Contents

A   *Abraham*

OUR 16ᵀᴴ PRESIDENT, Abraham Lincoln, was the leader of the United States during the difficult years of the Civil War. He saw himself as a self-taught, self-made man. He knew little about his ancestors, nor did he care to know about them. Neither did he care to talk about his early life: "... it is a great piece of folly to attempt to make anything out of my early life," he told the *Chicago Tribune* in 1860.

He did, however, know the true story of the grandfather for whom he had been named. The senior Abraham Lincoln, who had heard much about the rich soil in Kentucky from his distant relative, Daniel Boone, had packed up his family and headed west. This very same grandfather had taken his three sons (including Thomas, father of our Abraham) to plant a cornfield one day and was attacked and killed by Native Americans who were not enthusiastic about sharing their land with farmers from the east.

The Indians fled, and eight-year-old Thomas was still kneeling beside his father's body when his older brother Mordecai spotted one last Indian sneaking up on the boy. Mordecai took careful aim at the silver necklace on the Indian's chest and killed him before he could kill Thomas. If not for that successful shot, there would be no life of Abraham Lincoln to write about. As it turned out, Thomas lived to grow into manhood, married Nancy Hanks and together they moved to a little farm in Kentucky called Sinking Spring. On February 12, 1809, they named their newborn son *Abraham,* with no middle name, after the child's long dead grandfather.

Abraham Lincoln worked the same hard life of his father and grandfather searching for better lives in the west.

$\mathcal{B}$ *Black Hawk War*

THE HISTORY OF Chief Black Hawk and his Sauk tribe is similar to other Native American stories of initial co-operation with settlers, followed by resistance to the loss of their lands, broken promises and ultimate defeat. Abraham Lincoln's experience in the Black Hawk War in 1832 coincided with the tribe being tricked off their native land in Illinois, forcing them to the west side of the Mississippi River.

Lincoln, needing a paying job, signed on for the war with other restless young men from the area and soon found he was so well-liked that he was elected their captain. Later, in 1848, he said that being elected captain was "a success which gave me more pleasure than any I have had since."

The war suited Lincoln just fine in that it required no fighting except, "...I had a good many bloody struggles with musquetoes (sic)". In fact, it is often recalled that when Lincoln's troops came upon one old Indian and threatened to kill him as a spy, Lincoln stepped up and defended the man. Recalling his own grandfather's murder at the hands of disgruntled Indians, Lincoln might have been expected to take revenge on this old man; but that would not be the Abraham Lincoln who built his life on friendships and forgiveness.

On May 27, 1832, Lincoln's company was mustered out, but Lincoln re-enlisted for twenty more days in the mounted company of Captain Elijah Iles. After one further enlistment, Lincoln finished his military duty on July10, at White River, Wisconsin. Unfortunately, two horses were stolen from the unit, and the two owners, Lincoln and his messmate George Harrison, faced the long walk home. The other men of their company, including John Todd Stuart, Lincoln's future law partner, took turns walking, riding and swapping stories with them as they made their way south. From Peoria, the two then paddled a canoe to Havana, and from there they walked cross- country to New Salem.

Lincoln's war experience was ended but the friendships he made would continue to be to his advantage as the years went by.

In the spring and summer of 1832, Abraham Lincoln was Captain of his militia unit fighting in the Black Hawk War.

C   *Civil War*

THE CIVIL WAR, also known as The War Between the States, began only 80 years after the American Revolutionary War ended. The war technically began with the firing on Fort Sumter in South Carolina, but had its roots in the very formation of our nation.

In the Declaration of Independence, Thomas Jefferson planned to include words about the equality of **all** people, including slaves brought here as cheap labor. However, those words were scratched out of his document, in order to secure enough southern votes to ratify the declaration. Thus, the argument over slavery was postponed, not resolved. In only a few short years, the country was hopelessly divided over the issue, followed by the southern states seceding from the Union to maintain their right to keep slaves.

The stage was set for war, with Lincoln being sworn in as President of the whole country, trying desperately to keep the Union together. When southern troops fired on Fort Sumter in April 1861, folks on both sides thought the war would be short-lived. However, battles raged on for four bloody years.

During those years, Abraham Lincoln aged with worry and sorrow. He walked a fine line throughout the war in his effort to keep the Northern states united. He dealt with criticism at every turn. He was either too much of an abolitionist, or not enough of one. He was either too soft-hearted or too-hardhearted. It is a testament to his political ability and determination that he was able to balance the interests of many while keeping the goal of the Union ever in the forefront. Being re-elected to a second term as President in the midst of the anguish and despair, is perhaps the greatest compliment he ever earned.

The cares of the Civil War were etched into the face of Abraham Lincoln during the four long years.

$\mathcal{D}$ *Debates*

ALL EYES WERE on Illinois in 1858, as the two contestants for the Illinois seat in the United States Senate seemed to embody the entire nation's concern over the issue of slavery. Abraham Lincoln opposed allowing slavery to spread into the western territories, and Stephen A. Douglas supported the right of the citizens in the territories to decide the question themselves. So while the race was only a small, state contest, it was in essence a national debate over slavery.

It was Lincoln's idea to have a series of debates in seven regions of the state prior to the election in November. While Lincoln preferred to give well thought out, carefully written speeches, he felt that the challenge of a series of debates would help clarify their different stands. As the debates began in Ottawa, Lincoln seemed to find it difficult to argue his points against the verbal skills of Judge Douglas.

But as the debates continued, Lincoln gained momentum, while Douglas tired and weakened. Both suffered from strained voices after speaking for hours at a time to crowds of thousands. Lincoln, however, appeared to do his best in the last two debates. At Quincy, his words took on a fierce focus and he clearly stated the fundamental issue of the campaign as being "the difference between the men who think slavery a wrong and those who do not think it wrong".

Then it was up to the people in the state to decide. When the votes were counted, the Republicans (and Lincoln) had won the popular vote, but they did not gain control of the state legislature. And since the legislators were the ones who selected the US Senator, it was the Democrat, Stephen A. Douglas who won the election and returned to six more years in the Senate.

Lincoln had lost another election. But he wrote a friend,

"I am glad I made the late race. It gave me a hearing on the great and durable question of the age, which I could have had in no other way: and though I now sink out of view, and shall be forgotten, I believe I have made some marks which will tell for the cause of civil liberty long after I am gone."

E   *Eighth Street*

ABRAHAM LINCOLN AND his wife Mary lived their first year of marriage in the Globe Tavern, a noisy stage coach stop on the west side of the square in Springfield, Illinois. Soon after baby Robert was born in their tiny room, they rented a house on Fourth Street, until the Reverend Dresser, who had performed their wedding, sold them his house on Eighth Street. This was the only home Lincoln ever owned.

The tiny one floor house was in easy walking distance of his office, the capitol, and the train station. When Eddie joined their family in 1846, the house was feeling a bit cramped. By the mid-1850's, the couple and their three boys, Robert, Willie and Tad (Eddie had died at the age of three) had completely outgrown the premises.

During these Springfield years, Lincoln was a busy lawyer, traveling the Eighth Judicial district handling law cases. He was gone for weeks in a row during the fall and spring circuits. This was the way many lawyers made their living, as there were too many lawyers in Springfield for the amount of work to be had. This was also how Abraham came to know so many people around the state, who supported him in his later political life.

So it was presumably Mary who made the plans and dealt with the builders who added a second story to their home, doubling their living space. The little house grew into a lovely two-story Greek Revival style home.

When Lincoln left Springfield in February, 1861, as the newly elected President of the United States, the family put their things in storage, gave their dog to a kind family, and rented out their home. They fully intended to return to their life in Springfield after their sojourn in Washington. And they fully intended to return to the house on Eighth Street that they had made their home.

In this home, the Lincoln family grew and prospered. It was here that Abraham played with his boys, milked the cow and stabled his horse. Here also he received the congratulations of friends and neighbors when he was elected President of the United States.

F   *Friends*

FRIENDS WERE AN important part of Abraham Lincoln's life. Nothing gave him more pleasure than leaning back in a chair, resting his feet up higher than his head, and telling stories with old friends. People who knew him soon forgot his gangly body, his mussed up hair and his clothes that never seemed to fit right. They came to love this gentle man, who liked everyone he met.

Abraham had a way of making enemies into friends. Back in New Salem days, a country bully challenged him to a wrestling match and won by an illegal move. But Lincoln held no grudge and soon won the man's respect, friendship and loyalty.

With other lawyers, Lincoln traveled the Eighth Judicial district of Illinois meeting the legal needs of people who lived outside of Springfield. These traveling lawyers spent long hours together in the courtrooms. Then they ate their meals together, joked together and even slept in the same beds together. Lincoln was able to see the humor in these situations, winning the admiration of his friends inside and outside the courtroom.

As President, Lincoln chose his cabinet carefully. He wanted men of diverse opinions so as to fairly represent the whole country. This meant, however, that some of the cabinet members did not agree with his policies. Some actively worked against achievement of his goals. Some were even rude to him. Lincoln ignored and soon forgot their little hurts and snubs, choosing to remember the good rather than the bad in people and turning enemies into friends.

The friendships that Lincoln made through the years were never forgotten. He wrote, *"The better part of one's life consists of friendships."*

G   *Generals*

THE CIVIL WAR was imminent. Both sides were gearing up for the conflict. Both sides needed a capable general to lead their armies. The United States Army asked Robert E. Lee to be their leader. Would he say yes?

Robert E. Lee was a graduate of the United States Military Academy at West Point and at one time was the Superintendent there. He had fought in the Mexican War and on the Texas frontier and saw himself a loyal American, related to George Washington through his marriage to Martha Washington's great-granddaughter. But he was also a Lee, of the Lee family of old Virginia, and he felt loyalty to his state as well as his country. In one of those pivotal moments in history, Lee chose to join the fight with his fellow Virginians against the United States Army. His decision changed the course of the next 4 years.

President Lincoln was now faced with the problem of finding a general who could fight the likes of Lee and win. The war years found him firing many generals who could not seem to get the job done. More than once, Lincoln threatened to literally add on to his role of Commander-in-Chief and become a General himself! In fact, one night, in 1862, Lincoln took a ship down the Potomac River to scout out possible landing sites for an impending attack on the rebel held Southern shore. He then amazed his accomplices by getting off the tugboat and walking the beach on the Virginia side in bright moonlight! He had proved to

unbelieving officers that such a landing was possible. The next day, Union soldiers entered Norfolk and received the city's surrender.

Union Generals McClellan, Pope, Burnside, Hooker and Meade came and went and the never-ending war dragged on. Finally, Lincoln's attention was drawn to General Ulysses S. Grant who was successfully leading his troops to victory at Vicksburg, Mississippi. In this cigar-smoking, tough-talking General from Galena, Illinois, Lincoln had finally found a general who would chase the confederates down to their final defeat.

H   *Herndon*

LINCOLN'S LAW PARTNER, William H. Herndon, referred to Abraham as Mr. Lincoln; but to Abraham, William Herndon was always Billy. About nine years younger than Lincoln, they became friends in Springfield while they both lived with Joshua Speed above his store. Later, Billy clerked in the office of Logan and Lincoln, and then joined Lincoln as his junior partner in the Lincoln Herndon office.

Some say that Herndon's life began on Lincoln's death, when the country beat a path to the door of the Lincoln Law office and found William, the self-appointed authority on Lincoln, willing and able to tell stories of the martyred president. To his credit, he did painstaking research on the life of his former partner. To his discredit, he enlarged on the stories and added his own interpretations. Stories of Lincoln's paternity, stories of Lincoln's romances, and stories of Lincoln's religious views all took on the weight of truth by Herndon's repeated tellings.

Herndon interviewed people who had known Lincoln in his New Salem days and even sought out folks who had known the Lincoln family back in Indiana and Kentucky. He wrote countless letters and gathered stories both for the speeches he gave and for a book he intended to write about his famous law partner. He soon found it necessary to reduce his law practice, due to his demanding speaking schedule in cities and towns across the state and country.

Ever in awe of his friend the President, Herndon has left the world valuable descriptions of Lincoln the lawyer, the storyteller, the father and the politician. However, his attitude toward Mary Lincoln was totally different. Their dislike was mutual. After Robert Lincoln confronted Herndon in person about the story of  Abraham's alleged romance with Ann Rutledge, both Robert and Mary refused to share their letters and papers with him.

With the help of Jesse W. Weik, Herndon's <u>Lincoln</u>, was first published in 1889 by a Chicago publisher who sold few copies and soon went out of business. A second publisher, D. Appleton and Company, published the book in 1892. By then, Herndon was dead, never having seen the final product for which he had labored over 20 years.

I *Illinois*

THE FIRST PERMANENT town in the Illinois region was Cahokia, founded in 1699, in an area abandoned by Native Americans who had developed their own huge settlement there and then mysteriously disappeared. Nearby, French priests founded Kaskaskia in 1703. This became the capital when Congress created the Illinois Territory, and selected Ninian Edwards as Territorial Governor. As Illinois filled with settlers from the bottom up, becoming a state in 1818, the capital was moved to Vandalia to be more centrally located.

By 1836, there was a desire to move the capital again to a larger town even further to the north. Several towns sought the honor of being the capital, including Jacksonville, Peoria, Alton and Springfield. At this time, Abraham Lincoln, still living in New Salem, was one of nine representatives from Sangamon County, famously known as The Long Nine, due to their great height. They averaged six feet tall, but Lincoln was the tallest at six feet four inches. Lincoln had been studying law and borrowing law books from his old army buddy John Todd Stuart and so was familiar with the growing town of Springfield and its desire to become the new capital.

Lincoln was already politically shrewd enough to lead the delegation as they traded political favors for votes on the capital question. When the final vote was taken, Springfield had won as capital and Lincoln had won a place in the hearts and minds of many influential Springfield residents. When he moved to Springfield the next spring, he was not a completely unknown commodity.

Lincoln arrived in Springfield on April 15, 1837, at the exact midpoint of his life. He was 28 years old and would die 28 years later on April 15, 1865. It was in Springfield that he married, raised his family, practiced law and became the man who could face a task "greater than that which rested on Washington."

Across from the Lincoln Herndon Law offices is the State Capitol building where Lincoln, the lawyer, presented many cases in front of the Supreme Court. Here he gave his "House Divided" speech as well.

J   *Jacksonville*

AFTER THE LINCOLN-DOUGLAS debates, Abraham Lincoln continued traveling the state and giving speeches. On February 11, 1859, he caught the morning train to Jacksonville where he was to give an evening speech for the Phi Alpha Literary fraternity of Illinois College. The literary society was offering a series of lectures to the Jacksonville community, for a nominal fee, in the hope of making some money for their fraternity.

Lincoln's early arrival allowed him time to see Jacksonville friends and pass the afternoon enjoyably. After dinner, he arrived at the meeting place to find a very small crowd had gathered for his speech. Undeterred, he spoke on "Discoveries, Inventions and Improvements", observing that "Young America" had the advantage over "Old Fogy" European nations not only in her ability to sow the seeds of inventions, but also by a patent system which "secured to the inventor, for a limited time, the exclusive use of his invention." Here the speech ends rather abruptly.

Lincoln had spoken for an hour on discoveries and inventions without ever mentioning his own patent, number 6469, obtained on May 22, 1849, for a device to lift stranded boats up and over sandbars and other obstructions. He himself had had several experiences navigating dangerously shallow waters in Illinois rivers. He had once carefully watched as workers pushed empty casks under a boat upon which he was sailing to buoy it up and over an obstacle. Others watched also but it was Lincoln who took the idea a step further. Working with a Springfield mechanic, he designed an apparatus attached to the sides of a boat which could conveniently be inflated as needed when faced with shallow water.

Though he took the model with him to Washington, DC and received the patent, the invention was never used. Perhaps that was why he neglected to mention it in his speech. It does, however, make him the only President ever to hold a patent.

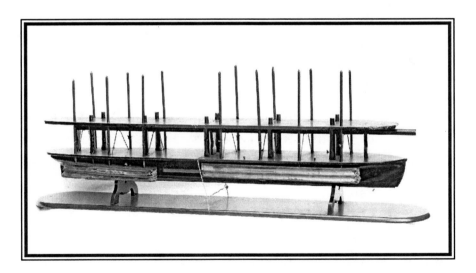

**Abraham Lincoln is the only President
to have held a patent on an invention.**

K   *Kidnaping*

KIDNAPING PRESIDENT LINCOLN was John Wilkes Booth's plan to help save the South. It had a very simple plot. The president often walked unguarded through the streets of Washington City, offering plenty of opportunities to kidnap him. Booth planned to whisk him away to Richmond where he would be held until the North agreed to exchange him for thousands of rebel prisoners-of-war who were desperately needed by the dwindling Confederate army. Then the South would be victorious.

Booth, the famous, handsome actor who had never been a soldier, dreamed he would become the hero who saved his country. The South would rise again! The applause would be worth any danger! It would be the greatest role of his career!

But then on April 9, 1865, General Robert E. Lee surrendered to General Grant at the Appomattox Courthouse. The War was over. Booth had missed his opportunity to kidnap the president and refill the southern army. President Lincoln stood on the balcony of the White House and spoke to a joyful crowd. He spoke of the long road that had been traveled and the road ahead to peace and reconciliation with the South. He praised the black Union soldiers for their courage on the battlefield and said that such brave soldiers deserved the right to vote in future United States elections.

John Wilkes Booth was in the crowd listening to the speech. His anger at the surrender was made greater by the thought that black men would be allowed the privilege of voting. It was too much for him. Suddenly, the plan to kidnap the President became a conspiracy to assassinate him as well as Vice President Johnson and Secretary of State Seward. When John Wilkes Booth decided to assassinate the President, the stage was set for the greatest performance of his career. He was going to be a hero.

In this unusual picture, the devil himself is whispering instructions into Booth's ear.

L   *Lawyer*

ONE THING LEADS to another and so it was with Abraham Lincoln. For in 1832, when Lincoln desperately needed a job and signed on for the Black Hawk War, he fortuitously met fellow soldiers who would later lead him into his legal and political careers.

After serving together in that war, Major John Todd Stuart encouraged Lincoln to read law by offering Abraham the use of his law books. Once Lincoln started to read the borrowed books, he didn't stop even when his friends worried that he was ruining his health! In 1837, Stuart invited Lincoln to share his law practice with him in Springfield. By then, Lincoln had served two terms in the state legislature and was poised to take on an important role in the political life in Springfield.

Stuart socialized in the best circles in Springfield. He provided Lincoln with ready access to this social whirl, which included his cousin Elizabeth Todd Edwards, who with her husband Ninian, son of the former Territorial Governor, hosted elegant parties. As luck would have it, Elizabeth had a visiting sister named Mary, of the eligible-to-marry-age, who soon met Abraham at one of their parties.

However, John Todd Stuart's interests leaned toward the political more than the legal, and when he was elected to a second term in Congress, Lincoln became law partners with the well-established Stephen T. Logan, who nurtured and honed Abraham's still developing legal skills. Lincoln and Logan later parted on friendly terms when Logan became partner with his own son, David. By then, Lincoln was himself a distinguished lawyer with aspirations of his own to run for Congress. Asking a young lawyer William H. Herndon to join him in practice, Lincoln entered a partnership that would last the rest of his life.

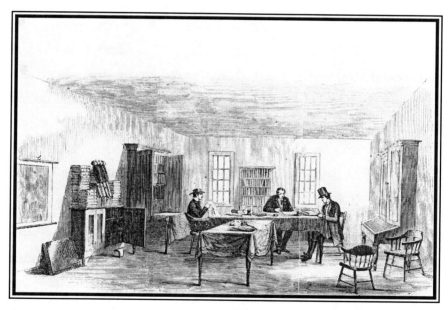

When Lincoln left to become President, he told Billy Herndon, "Give our clients to understand that the election of a President makes no change in the firm of Lincoln and Herndon. If I live I'm coming back some time, and then we'll go right on practicing law as if nothing happened."

M Mary Lincoln

THE EXCEPTIONAL LIFE of Abraham Lincoln's wife, Mary Ann Todd, can be divided quite nicely into three parts of approximately the same length.

1818-1842

Born to wealth in Lexington, Kentucky, Mary enjoyed the pampered life, with house slaves to meet any and all needs. Her life changed abruptly when her mother died, her father remarried, and she lost her favored status. As soon as possible, Mary fled to the home of her sister Elizabeth Edwards in Springfield, Illinois, seeking independence and opportunity.

1842-1865

Marrying a future president was said to be Mary's girlhood ambition, and on November 4, 1842, she wed Abraham Lincoln believing in his potential. They shared a love for each other and a love of politics. Four sons and many frugal years later, life took them to the White House where Mary tried to live up to her own great expectations. She redecorated the neglected house, held elegant parties, and hoped to be accepted by Washington society. Behind the scenes, Mary visited soldiers in nearby hospitals, and distributed blankets and clothing to homeless, escaped slaves who filled the back streets of Washington, DC with poverty and hope.

1865-1882

The last third of Mary's life found her wandering from Chicago, to New York to Europe, searching for a place that felt like home. Her husband and three of her sons were dead. Her living son, Robert, saw her distress, and urged the sanity hearings which found her incapable of caring for herself. However, after only a few months in the sanitarium, Mary was released to live in her sister's home in  Springfield where her wedding had been held so many years before. After a final trip to Europe, she returned once again to Elizabeth's home. Here she died in July of 1882, joining Abraham, Eddie, Willie and Tad in Oak Ridge Cemetery.

$\mathcal{N}$ *New Salem*

MANY PEOPLE GO to college to become educated. Abraham Lincoln went to a small town on the Illinois frontier for his education. For it was in New Salem that Lincoln established himself when he came of age and it was there that he grew from a man of brawn to a man of brains.

Lincoln the rail splitter, the farmer, the builder, the wrestler, the river rat, came to New Salem in 1831 as a likable, gangly, rather shy young man seeking his place in the world. He left New Salem in 1837, a well-read, self-educated man who had assumed an influential position in the town and in the state legislature. Perhaps it was the newness of the small town atmosphere that enabled him to become a leader. Everyone was similarly poor and uneducated, allowing those with the will to rise. Perhaps it was the basic values of the people which gave confidence to the most unlikely of characters playing on the town's stage.

New Salem, Illinois was a hopeful little community, depending on the Sangamon River and its mills for growth and survival. For only a few years, those hopes brought settlers and vigor to this corner of the Midwest. It is almost as if the town came into being to provide a nurturing home for

Lincoln during his years there, because not long after he left, the town completely disappeared. Yes, the log houses were even moved to new locations, leaving only one original house to weather the years.

It was here that Lincoln, the storekeeper, taught himself the rudiments of grammar, the basics of mathematics, the techniques of surveying, and the essentials of law. He accomplished all that while nurturing friendships, gaining self-confidence, and acquiring political savvy. "Lincoln's Alma Mater" is an apt phrase to describe his years in this log cabin village.

The Berry-Lincoln Store

O

Our American Cousin

ABRAHAM LINCOLN ENJOYED going to the theater, especially during his presidential years. He loved the jokes in the comedies, the carefree tunes in the musicals and the life-and-death drama of Shakespeare. He also enjoyed the hours of peace which going to the theater provided. In those moments, there were no questions to be answered, no favors to be granted, and no lists of injured soldiers to ache over.

On April 14, 1865, Abraham and Mary decided to celebrate the end of the war by going to the Ford Theater to see the silly comedy of errors called *Our American Cousin*. Though the President had been warned to stay out of large crowds where security was difficult due to rumors of a likely kidnaping attempt, Lincoln would not hear of it. He was setting the example that life would return to normal now that peace had been attained.

That night, John Wilkes Booth, an actor who knew the Ford Theater well, had in mind much more than simply kidnaping the president. He and two friends were going to kill President Lincoln, Vice-President Andrew Johnson and Secretary of State William Seward at the very same moment, 10:15 p.m, thus throwing the government into such disarray that Confederate dreams could still be realized.

Booth carried out his portion of the plot. He crept into the President's private box and shot him in the back of the head. At the same exact moment, another accomplice nearly beat Secretary Seward to death in his home. The third accomplice walked the streets alone all that night, unable to force himself to murder the Vice President.

After shooting the President, Booth leapt to the stage breaking an ankle in his fall. The dying President was carried across the street to a house owned by William Petersen. In a back room, Lincoln fought for every breath until the next morning. About 7 a.m., Lincoln breathed his last and his friend Edwin Stanton tenderly spoke the touching final words, "Now he belongs to the ages."

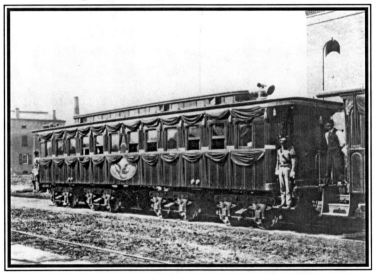

The funeral train carried Abraham Lincoln back to his beloved Springfield for burial. However, his was not the only casket on the train. Willie's small casket accompanied him. The train followed the same route that had brought the Lincoln family to Washington over four years earlier, this time stopping often for grieving throngs to reverently pass the coffin.

$\mathcal{P}$ *Proclamation*

PRESIDENT LINCOLN BELIEVED that over time people would see how wrong slavery was and would simply stop keeping slaves. He believed that if slavery were not allowed to spread into the western territories that gradually the "peculiar institution" would disappear throughout the whole United States. His focus, therefore, in the beginning of the Civil War was mostly on reuniting the states and keeping the Union together.

Yet, as the war dragged on, Lincoln came to believe that some action must be taken to speed up the process of ending slavery. Under his war powers, he, as President, could do certain things not allowed during peace time. So, in 1862, he wrote a document called The Emancipation Proclamation, which would free the slaves in the states in rebellion against the United States.

Before the Proclamation was even signed, many people praised him for finally doing the right thing. Yet some scolded him for only freeing the slaves in the rebel states. Many feared that the Proclamation would tip the balance in the Border States and cause them to secede also. Others thought he had hurt the whole Republican Party by issuing such a proclamation. And some argued that not one slave was really freed, because once the war was over, the courts would declare the Proclamation unconstitutional.

Previously, Lincoln had tried to think of other ways to free the slaves. He had suggested three amendments to the Constitution. He had suggested that the United States pay bonds to states which outlawed slavery. He had suggested paying masters to free their slaves. He had suggested paying freed slaves to go live in a colony outside the United States. Yet nothing had happened.

Finally, Lincoln felt compelled to take action and make a decision. On January 1, 1863, he signed the Emancipation Proclamation, saying, *"I never, in my life, felt more certain that I was doing right, than I do in signing this paper."*

Q

Quarrels

WHILE THE QUARREL between the North and South occupied most of Lincoln's time, another quarrel was brewing and could not be ignored. This time, the quarrel was in Minnesota, between the Sioux Indians and the settlers who were heading west in droves.

The Sioux had signed a treaty with the United States government giving up most of their native land in return for money. But the promised payments never came and the Indians became increasingly desperate. The Department of Indian Affairs saw their plight and begged the U.S. government to quickly send the money for the now landless and starving Indians. They could see that trouble was brewing. Yet nothing happened. As a last resort, a few young braves raided a farm in Acton, Minnesota, hoping to steal some eggs. They unfortunately ended up killing five settlers. This lit an uprising which eventually killed 350 settlers.

Lincoln assigned General Pope, who had just been defeated at the Second Battle of Bull Run, to stop the fighting. The General took his revenge out on the Indians, capturing 1500 men, women and children. The military commission scheduled 303 of them to die, and preparations were made for the largest hanging ever to be seen.

Abraham, who was never fond of violence, insisted on seeing for himself the list of arrested Indians and their crimes. He carefully studied the difficult names, searching for ones who had been convicted of the worst crimes. He reduced the number to be hanged to 39.

In the end, on December 26, 1862, 38 Indian men were hanged in the largest execution in American history, (one more man was pardoned at the last minute). In the Presidential election two years later, Lincoln lost many votes in Minnesota. He was told he would have had more votes if he had hanged more Indians. But Abraham Lincoln was unable to think of buying votes with lives and felt satisfied he had done the right thing.

R   *Robert*

THE ELDEST OF Abraham Lincoln's four boys was the only one to live into manhood. Robert was born on August 1, 1843, when Abraham and Mary still lived in the Globe Tavern. *"Bob is short and low"* wrote Lincoln to his friend Joshua Speed, taking after the Todd side of the family for whom he had been named. With his arrival, the Lincoln family outgrew their one room residence, and moved to a house on Fourth Street.

The young Lincoln family, now including a second son, Eddie, journeyed together to Washington, DC, when Abraham was elected to Congress in 1847. But the boys soon left with their mother to spend time in Lexington, Kentucky with Mary's father and his family. Thus Robert began a close relationship with the Todd family that lasted throughout his lifetime.

Robert was the son who cared about social graces. He was a meticulous dresser, an excellent dancing partner and he practiced manners for which he became well known throughout his life. In many ways, he was the opposite of his father who cared little for his personal appearance, and was known to dance "in the worst way" according to his wife. But

Robert learned, as the country did also, that appearances count less than character and Robert's love and respect for his father grew as Lincoln's life unfolded.

Robert's life was filled with sorrow, from the deaths of his three brothers and father, to the death of his own son, Abraham II, and to the distress of watching his mother's grief in the years following Abraham's assassination. Yet he maintained his ability to be his own person in a world that tended to see him primarily as "Abe Lincoln's son". He practiced law and business, was the Secretary of War, and the Ambassador to England. He socialized with the elite of Chicago and when he died, he chose to be buried in Arlington Cemetery, the only Lincoln not buried in Springfield, Illinois.

S

Springfield

IN 1837, ABRAHAM Lincoln moved to Springfield, Illinois, in time to watch the town grow itself into the state capital. He was there to watch the oxen, ten or twelve to a team, pull the heavy loads of buff colored stone from the quarry south of Cotton Hill up Sixth Street to the square where the building of the State Capitol was underway.

It was in Springfield that Lincoln courted a pretty socialite named Mary Todd, who eased Abraham's nervousness by talking enough for both of them. They came from very different backgrounds but they shared a love of politics. It was enough to make a marriage and on November 4, 1842, they wed in the parlor of her sister's home at Second and Edwards Streets. Four sons were born to them in Springfield.

It was in Springfield, in 1858, that Lincoln took the short walk across the street from his law office to the capitol building and made a giant leap into national prominence, when he delivered his "House Divided" speech. It was in Springfield that he set the stage for his stand against slavery and for unity by saying, *"I believe this government cannot endure, permanently half slave and half free."*

And it was at the train station in Springfield that Lincoln said farewell to his friends of many years on a rainy February 11, 1861, never to return alive.

"Here I have lived a quarter of a century, and have passed from a young to an old man. Here my children have been born, and one is buried. I now leave, not knowing when or whether ever I may return, with a task before me greater than that which rested upon Washington ... I bid you an affectionate farewell."

T *Tad*

THOMAS LINCOLN WAS the youngest of the four boys born to Abraham and Mary. When he was born, Abraham thought the baby's large head and small body resembled a tadpole and the nickname "Tad" stuck. Tad was born into a family who believed that the best discipline was very little discipline. Therefore, the Lincoln boys were usually allowed to do as they pleased.

For Tad this meant years of fun and freedom with his nearest brother, Willie, both in Springfield and in Washington. They became a famous and feared duo who could wreak havoc in their father's law office, drive their pet nanny goats through the crowds in the White House and set up a fort on the White House roof.

Life changed drastically for Tad in February of 1862 when Willie died. Suddenly his best friend and his carefree life were both gone. His distraught mother forbade children to come play and gave away Willie's favorite toys. Tad acknowledged that the time had come for him to grow up.

He spent the next years of his life growing closer and closer to his father, following him to the telegraph office in the War Department, standing at his side as he addressed crowds,

F. Weisbrod phot.   Frankfurt a/M.

watching as his father sat for an artist and walking at his side through Richmond at the end of the war. And then his father was gone too.

After Abraham's death in 1865, Tad and his mother left the White House and moved from place to place searching for happiness. For a while they lived in Chicago, where Tad finally decided he was old enough to dress himself and attend school. He studied with a speech teacher to correct a lisp that had made him difficult to understand by those who did not know him well. The mother and son also found that traveling throughout Europe provided some distraction from their sorrows, and Tad was reportedly growing into a handsome manhood.

Then Tad himself caught a cold that progressed into pneumonia and he died in the summer of 1871. The eldest son, Robert, was left to bury his last brother in Oak Ridge Cemetery in Springfield, as he had buried his father and Willie. Mary was heartbroken and unable to attend any of their burials.

$\mathcal{U}$ *Union*

IN 1861, BEFORE the Civil War started, there were 34 states in the union which made up the United States of America. Then, southern states began seceding from the union to form their own government which they called The Confederate States of America. This government had its first headquarters in Montgomery, Alabama, and then in Richmond, Virginia. The President of the Confederacy was Jefferson Davis, a former United States Senator who had served at the time Abraham Lincoln served in the House of Representatives.

Lincoln believed that the Union of all the states was *"the last, best hope on earth"*, and struggled mightily to achieve reunion by winning the Civil War. Actually, he believed that seceding from the Union was illegal so he was very careful not to recognize the Confederacy as a legitimate country. He rarely referred to Jefferson Davis as the President of the Confederacy because he believed there was no such job since there was no such country. In his Second Inaugural Address (photo), Lincoln referred to "one of" the parties in the conflict, carefully not calling them The South or The Confederacy.

As the war drew to a close, Lincoln believed more than ever that no revenge should be taken against the defeated army or the prisoners of war. Because he felt that both the North and the South were responsible for the war in different ways, he wanted all the soldiers to be allowed to go home and rebuild their lives knowing that this would in turn rebuild the strength of the Union. Each man should be allowed to keep his horse for spring planting. Each state should be allowed to elect congressmen with full participation in the political life in Washington. Lincoln planned for the peacemaking as carefully as for the war-making.

On April 10th, when a band was serenading the victorious leader outside the White House, he said, *"I have always thought "Dixie" one of the best tunes I ever heard... I now request the band to favor me with its performance."* In ways small and large, Lincoln was setting the stage for an amicable reunion of the two sides of the conflict.

$\mathcal{V}$ *Victory*

IN APRIL OF 1865, the War Between the States drew to a close. Abraham Lincoln, ever involved with the proceedings, rode to City Point and boarded the *River Queen* for talks with Generals Grant and Sherman. They discussed strategy; how the noose of Union soldiers was tightening around the remaining Army of Northern Virginia led by General Robert E. Lee. The end was nearing for the starving, weary rebels. Lincoln expressed fear that the clever General Lee might yet escape with his army as he had so many times before. This time, however, the trap held and Lee's army had no where to turn.

On April 9, 1865, Generals Grant and Lee met at the Appomattox Courthouse to discuss surrender terms. Robert Lincoln, as an aide to Grant, witnessed the remarkable event. Grant, who held General Lee in high regard, knew how difficult this moment would be for him. He wanted to make the surrender as easy as possible on the southerners knowing that they were soon going to be living side by side as fellow citizens.

General Lee was surprised by the generous terms the Union offered. The officers could keep their weapons and the soldiers could keep their horses and mules. They were all free to go home and begin a life of peace. Lee could hardly believe his ears. After all the hatred and violence, was there really to be no taking of prisoners? No hangings? No punishment?

Signing the peace treaty was not so much an end of war as it was the beginning of peace. President Lincoln had made it clear to General Grant that the terms of the peace treaty must be generous so that the peacetime that followed would be generous also.

Before they left the courthouse, Lee whispered to Grant that his troops were literally starving. Grant issued the necessary orders and the confederates were served Union rations along with the news that the war was over.

Then, with a final, quiet salute, the generals acknowledged their great respect for each other. The War Between the States was over.

W

Willie

KNOWN AS THE "good" boy of the two White House ragamuffins, Willie was older than Tad and more serious. He was thoughtful and tried to teach Tad right from wrong. Sometimes described as a mama's boy, Willie was less hardy than his younger brother, a serious problem in the era before modern medicines wiped out most childhood diseases.

Among many gifts from friends and well-wishers, the Lincoln boys received a pet pony to ride on the White House lawn. Riding on a cold and blustery day in January of 1862 probably aggravated illnesses already building in their bodies. Both boys became dangerously ill, but it was Willie who could not muster the strength needed to overcome the fever.

Abraham Lincoln sat up nights with his dangerously ill sons, weakening his own health and despairing. Then on February 20, after their friend Bud Taft visited, Willie died. Abraham and Mary were devastated to lose a second cherished son. In her grief, Mary took to her room but Abraham stayed close to Tad to nurse him to health.

After the funeral, Willie's casket was laid in a temporary vault on a stormy day, with Abraham and Robert the only family members present. The plan was to return to Springfield and properly bury him there, next to his brother Eddie, when Lincoln's presidency ended. Instead, Willie's little casket rode the funeral train with his father's casket, on its long journey through crowds of mourners along the 1700 miles to Springfield after Lincoln was assassinated in April, 1865.

Willie and his father were buried side by side in Oak Ridge Cemetery.

eXecutive Branch

AN IMPORTANT PART of the Executive Branch of the government of the United States is the President's cabinet. The cabinet members head up departments such as Defense, Agriculture, and Energy, and they come together to advise the President on issues large and small.

In Lincoln's era, there were 9 cabinet members. As President Lincoln chose the members of his cabinet, he surprised many people by choosing people who didn't always agree with him on issues. In fact, many violently disagreed with him. Some thought that *they* should have been elected president instead of him. Some even treated the president with disrespect.

Friends of Mr. Lincoln suggested that he should have chosen people to be on his team who agreed with him on all the issues. But President Lincoln was smarter than many people knew at the time. He knew that it is good to have diversity of opinions. He knew that he wanted intelligent people surrounding him discussing all sides of every problem. He knew that to have a fair and balanced government, he needed to have a fair and balanced cabinet.

The President remembered that when he was just a young boy back home in Indiana, he had to carry two big pumpkins while he rode horse back. They were awkward and heavy. He solved the problem by carrying one on each side of the horse which gave him the balance he needed to ride smoothly. He compared his cabinet members to balancing those pumpkins long ago. By having a wide variety of opinions represented on his cabinet, he said, "I can ride now. I've got a pumpkin in each end of my bag."

The balance Lincoln strove so hard to achieve paid off with good decisions made by people who studied every side of every argument and sought what was best for the country.

$\mathcal{Y}$ *Yellow Dog*

CATS! DOGS! GOATS! Horses! Turkeys! Yes, the tender-hearted Lincoln family loved a wide variety of pets over the years.

Abraham Lincoln's compassion for animals began in his youth. One story tells of Lincoln standing up to a group of boys who were torturing a large turtle by heaping hot coals on its back, to see if the soft critter inside would wriggle out. Lincoln was big enough and strong enough to stop such shenanigans.

Stories of anti-cruelty continue into his parenthood. Apparently, the Lincoln boys were once trying to train their dogs to stand up and walk on their hind feet by stringing them up with ropes to force them into upright posture. Abnormal amounts of howling alerted Mr. Lincoln who may have threatened his own boys with a barrel stave (but one doubts he would have done more than threaten with it.)

The tales of pet goats pulling the Lincoln boys in a wagon through the White House are well known. A lesser known story involves a Christmas turkey whom Tad befriended. He then convinced his father that the bird should not become dinner but instead should be reprieved with a note penned by the President himself. Jack, the turkey, lived to enjoy his life on the White House grounds, dutifully trailing behind Tad and harassing the encamped soldiers.

This not-very-handsome, yellow-haired mutt named Fido endeared himself to the family about the time Lincoln was elected President. With all the photographers around, it appears that the winsome pet calmly posed along with the parents and children. The boys begged to bring the dog with them to Washington but Abraham convinced them that the dog would be much happier staying in Illinois with the John Roll family who had boys about the ages of Tad and Willie.

The Lincoln family could not take Fido with them when they left for Washington so a special portrait was taken instead.

Z   *Zouaves*

THE ZOUAVE UNIFORM craze began after Captain George B. McClellan admired the colorful uniforms of the French /Algerian soldiers while serving as an observer in the far away Crimean War in the 1850's. When he returned with tales of the skill and bravery of the French/Algerian soldiers, the uniforms became popular across the United States. They sometimes served as a status symbol, being worn by well-trained, veteran troops who took pride in their drill competitions and bayonet expertise.

Handsome, young Elmer Ellsworth found his calling as drill master of the US Zouave Cadets of Chicago. Previously, he had been a clerk in Lincoln's office, and after the Presidential election, he rode the train with the Lincoln family to Washington, DC. He became a great favorite of Willie and Tad as well as Abraham and Mary.

The Civil War had barely begun when Ellsworth's new corps of Fire Zouaves (volunteer firemen from New York City) marched into DC to defend the Capital. On May 24, 1861, his Zouaves crossed the Potomac to seize the rebel held town of Alexandria, Virginia. On their way to the telegraph office, Ellsworth spied a huge confederate flag atop the Marshall

House Hotel and immediately announced, "Boys, we must have that flag!" They charged in, hauled down the flag and as Elmer himself carried it down the stairs, the angry innkeeper mortally wounded him in the chest.

The Lincoln family was devastated and ordered that Ellsworth's body lie in state in the East Room of the White House. His death inspired more Zouave units to sprout up wearing similarly flashy attire. Tad Lincoln acquired the confederate flag that Elmer had captured, and loved to display it from the windows of the White House, to the dismay of some loyal Union folks.

Tad and Willie begged for Zouave uniforms of their own with a soldier doll to match. Once, while playing with the doll, Tad burst into a cabinet meeting and announced that Jack was to be shot for falling asleep on guard duty. His indulgent father immediately wrote out a pardon for the doll and thus spared his "life".

Mary Lincoln from A to Z

By

Betty Carlson Kay

Table of Contents

A   *Adolescence*

"CLEAR BLUE EYES, long lashes, light brown hair with a glint of bronze, and a lovely complexion" made Mary Todd an attractive adolescent, in the words of her niece, Katherine Helm. She could talk and flirt with the rest of the girls in Lexington, Kentucky in the 1830's, but underneath her outer charm and vivaciousness, there was a sad young lady, plagued with feelings of abandonment. Her precious mother had died when she was only seven, her father had a new wife who demanded the attention Mary thought should be hers, and now they even had a new home. Yes, the new Todd house on Main Street had enough rooms to accommodate the growing family, yet Mary never felt at "home" in it.

So the unhappy teenager found love and acceptance at a boarding school. The Mentelle School in Lexington was not far away and Mary could have easily been a day student but it was mutually agreeable to have Mary live at the school during the week and return home only on the weekends. Here, Mary found challenging studies like French, grammar, arithmetic and geography to stimulate her quick mind. This strenuous curriculum appealed to both Mary and to her father who wanted his favorite daughter to be able to carry on intelligent conversations. Instead of the usual 4 years of schooling for girls, Mary attended 10 years. This extra education made her attractive to some of her peers and intimidating to others.

In 1835, an invitation to visit her eldest sister Elizabeth, who had married Ninian Edwards and moved to Springfield, Illinois, provided an opportunity to get even further away from her stepmother. When Mary visited Springfield again in 1837, her life was put on a collision course with Abraham Lincoln's life as he arrived in Springfield the same year.

Young Mary Todd as painted by her niece, Katherine Helm.

$\mathcal{B}$ *Beaux*

IN 1839, MARY returned to Springfield to live with her sister Elizabeth and her husband Ninian Edwards, a man actively involved with local politics. Mary was soon the center of attention in the young, social set which gathered at the Edward's home. This coterie consisted of the elite of the town, with lawyers, judges and wealthy gentlemen in attendance upon the attractive ladies.

At dances, receptions and parties, Mary was a fluent, entertaining conversationalist who had the instinct for just the right word. Her blue eyes sparkled, her dimples delighted, and she found herself surrounded by many beaux. "She is the very creature of excitement you know and never enjoys her self more than when in society and surrounded by a company of many friends," James C. Conkling wrote of Mary in 1840.

One beau in particular drew much attention, as he and Mary made an attractive couple in size and shape. Stephen A. Douglas courted Mary at parties, plays and entertainments. Mary enjoyed his wit and style, yet felt at odds with his politics. Mary was a Whig supporter and everyone knew it. She was not in agreement with Douglas's Democratic Party leanings and the courtship went no where. To the astonishment of some and the dismay of others, Mary felt herself pulled more and more to a tall, rather homely man nine years her elder, who seemed uncomfortable with the social set in which he had found himself. He was becoming a well known lawyer and his friends thought he had great potential. But he often became tongue-tied around women and found dancing challenging. Mary kept her sparkling eyes on this interesting man named Abraham Lincoln.

C

Courtship

AS MARY AND Abraham began their courting, Springfield society watched with interest. What an odd couple they were! He was tall, she was short. He was thin, she tended to plump. He was a country boy and she was of the social elite. He tended toward depression and melancholy, she was excitable and hot-tempered. It surprised everyone when their friendship blossomed.

They did have several things in common. They both liked talking politics and they enjoyed reading and reciting poetry. Just when things seemed to be going well for them, the couple ended their relationship for reasons still questioned by historians. Their break-up occurred on the first of the year 1841, known thereafter to Lincoln as The Fatal First. Some say that Mary's relatives strongly objected to the match because they were sure that Abraham could never provide for her in the way she was accustomed. The split was painful to both of them, with Lincoln going into a deep depression that lasted months. Of course, he continued with his obligations in the Statehouse and in his law practice, but the spark had gone out of both of them.

When friends arranged their reunion, politics again played a role in their courtship. It had to do with some letters to the editor of the Sangamo Journal. Lincoln often wrote opinion letters to the newspaper in his folksy, witty way and most everyone in town could guess the author. But this time, Mary followed up with letters of her own in a similar style. Unfortunately, the target of the letters, James Shields, the State Auditor, did not take kindly to the attacks which he felt were insulting to him personally. Lincoln took the blame for the letters and Mr. Shields then challenged him to a duel. After going all the way to Missouri where dueling was legal, friends were able to stop the fight before it even began and they all returned to Springfield safe and sound. For taking all the blame, Lincoln became Mary's hero, her knight in shining armor. There was no stopping the romance now no matter what anyone thought.

$\mathcal{D}$ *Dresses*

DRESSING WELL WAS always an important part of Mary's life. As a child in Kentucky, Mary could bat her eyes and her father would provide her with beautiful dresses for special occasions. As a young wife, married to a man with a good income, Mary could afford nice fabric and fancy ribbons to make her dresses extra special. Of course at this time, she was doing much of the sewing on the dresses herself, no small feat considering the ten yards of fabric in the skirt alone.

When the Lincoln family arrived in Washington City as the First Family, Mary felt it her duty to dress the part of the First Lady of the land. She was determined to dress as well as the established social elite. Even before the inauguration, Mary made a shopping trip to New York City to purchase the best fabrics, the best trims and the best accessories. No one would be able to call her a country hick!

Next, she needed a seamstress and friends recommended Elizabeth Keckley. Mary was at once impressed with Lizzie and together they produced opulent gowns of the latest fashion. "I must dress in costly materials," Mary said to Mrs. Keckley. "The people scrutinize every article I wear with critical curiosity. The very fact of having grown up in the West, subjects me to more searching observation."

After Willie's death in 1862, and again after her husband's assassination, Mary dressed herself in the Victorian style of Widow's Weeds. Covered in black crepe from head to toe, Mary tried to hide her grief from the world but became a recognizable figure walking down the streets of Chicago and European cities.

Mrs. Lincoln. No 7.

E Elizabeth

ELIZABETH WAS THE eldest sister in the Todd family. As such, she assumed much of the responsibility for her younger siblings upon the death of their mother in 1825. Five years older than Mary, Elizabeth was 12 when their mother died. Feeling abandoned, Mary looked to her for love and nurture although Elizabeth was of an age to still need a mother herself. When Elizabeth married Ninian Edwards, Mary once again felt abandoned. No wonder that Mary went to visit and then live with the couple in Springfield as soon as possible. Again, Elizabeth assumed the role of mother figure, this time by planning and chaperoning social events wherein Mary could meet potential beaux. When Mary's choice of a suitor did not meet Elizabeth's expectations, she played the role of a controlling mother and interfered with the romance. Elizabeth was only able to postpone the inevitable, however, and when Mary and Abraham announced their intention to wed with or without family approval, Elizabeth and Ninian insisted on hosting the wedding at their home.

The sisters were not close during the early years of the Lincoln marriage although they lived in the same town. Mary knew that her sister did not approve of her husband and her feelings were hurt. Some of the hurt disappeared during the White House years and when Willie died in 1862, Elizabeth came to be with Mary for several weeks.

Mary and Elizabeth saw little of each other after the assassination. In 1875, the Cook County Court deemed Mary incapable of caring for herself and sent her to live in a home in Batavia, Illinois. Mary had no intention of staying in this restrictive environment and once again, Elizabeth came to her rescue writing, "Had I been consulted, I would have remonstrated earnestly against the steps taken." So it was that Elizabeth welcomed Mary back to the home she had been married in almost 40 years earlier. After a final trip to Europe, Mary died in Elizabeth's home on July 16, 1882.

𝓕 *Father*

MARY'S FATHER WAS Robert Smith Todd, a country gentleman whose family had deep roots back to the American Revolution. Theirs was a large extended family and no one was surprised when he married his cousin Eliza Parker.

By this time, the wealth of the Kentucky woods had provided them with gracious living standards. Robert was an influential landowner active in politics which often meant spending time away from his family. His children grew up under the care of loving slaves who tended the babies, polished the silver and cooked the meals. Stately horses and carriages were part of their everyday life.

The death of his wife left him both lonely and overwhelmed with six young children. He soon married Betsey Humpheys and began a second family with her. They had nine children to add to his previous brood. In this very full house, Mary always wanted more of her father's attention than she got. Robert showed his special affection for Mary in little ways. He engaged her in conversations not usually shared with children, he allowed her to go to school longer than other girls in that era and he continued to give her special gifts even as an adult.

Mary named her first born son after her handsome father who soon came to visit his namesake. Recognizing that she had not married a wealthy man, Robert generously gave her a yearly allowance of $120 and 80 acres of land nearby. He also gave some legal business to Abraham whom he respected.

Mary's father died in the cholera epidemic that spread like wildfire through Lexington in 1849. Mary was devastated but soon other deaths followed in its wake. Her adored Grandmother Parker died, freeing her slaves as she had promised. Then, little Eddie sickened and died before his fourth birthday.

And so it was that Robert Todd Lincoln carried his mother's family name, reminding her of the father she so admired.

G *Grandmother*

MARY LINCOLN LOVED each of her four sons with a passion, but when she became a Grandmother, she experienced the special love familiar to grandparents around the globe.

Robert was the only Lincoln son who lived to have children of his own. In 1868, he married Mary Harlan whose father was a Senator from Iowa. Upon marriage her name became Mary Lincoln as well. In 1869, their first born entered the world. It was a girl! What a happiness in a family that specialized in boys! Far across the Atlantic on her European tour, Mary was sure that the baby would be named for the maternal grandmother so as not to have a third Mary Lincoln in the family. But the proud parents decided to name their daughter after her mother and her paternal grandmother. To avoid confusion, this new Mary Lincoln was nicknamed Mamie. Returning home from abroad in 1871, Mary couldn't wait to see her first grandchild. When a grandson was born in 1873, he was named Abraham, but nicknamed Jack. The third and final child received the less confusing name, Jessie.

Unfortunately, as the years passed Mary saw very little of her three beautiful grandchildren. When Grandmother Mary entered Bellevue Place after she was judged incapable of caring for herself, Robert and Mamie came to visit every week. No matter how angry Mary was at Robert for his role in the insanity trial, she was always happy when Mamie visited.

When once again declared able to care for herself, Mary fled to Pau, France, far away from her offensive son, Robert. Living abroad meant not being near her grandchildren but they were never far from her thoughts. Gifts and greetings were sent to them from France, Italy, Scotland and Canada.

In 1881, Mary returned to Springfield a white-haired, ailing woman. Robert sought reconciliation and brought twelve-year-old Mamie with him for a visit, knowing that Mary's maternal love would win him back to her good graces.

Mary died before she was forced to endure the death of yet another Lincoln child. For in 1890, seventeen-year-old Abraham died of blood poisoning while his family was living in England. For a while, he joined the Lincoln family in Oak Ridge Cemetery before finally resting with his father in  Arlington National Cemetery.

$\mathcal{H}$ *Hostess*

MARY LOVED NOTHING more than being the hostess of a big party. The bigger the better was her motto. In Springfield, in 1857, Mary hosted a levee for 500 invited guests in their little home on 8th Street. Two parlors and a dining room allowed the guests barely enough space to mingle and nibble on party food. Crowded parties such as this one were known as "squeezes" by the locals. Today they might be called an open house. The parties at the Lincoln home were deemed the best in town with Abraham's magnetic personality making each guest feel welcome. The little Lincoln boys enjoyed livening up the events as only they could, while Bob quietly improved his social skills. Since Abraham and Mary did not drink alcoholic beverages, guests were offered coffee or water. If strawberries were in season, the party might feature trays of berries stacked high in the middle of the dining table.

Arriving in Washington, Mary knew that being the First Lady meant being the First Hostess as well. She considered the usual four-hour formal state dinners boring and expensive. She preferred to entertain in a more democratic style by issuing invitations to hundreds of friends and dignitaries for parties beginning at 9 o'clock at night. The First Couple would make their grand entrance about 10, and doors would be opened to the banquet hall around midnight. The feasting and partying would end around dawn as exhausted guests said their farewells. After one such party, a Washington journalist wrote of Mary, "Her hospitality is only equaled by her charity, and her graceful deportment by her goodness of heart."

Mary chose the Solferino pattern made by the Haviland Company as the Official White House china.

I   *Illness*

MARY LINCOLN'S VIVACIOUS personality hid the sad fact that she was not a healthy woman. She had been plagued with migraine headaches since her youth. These headaches had the power to send her to bed in a darkened room for two or three days. Words like eager, energetic, loving and flirtatious described her on days when she was feeling well but when she was not, then words like jealous, spiteful, and hysterical described her actions.

Her illnesses increased as she aged. Bearing four sons without aid of modern medicine took its toll on Mary as on all women of the 1800's. High blood pressure and diabetes contributed to her erratic behavior. Painful arthritis plagued her. In the White House, mood swings were evident early and temper tantrums were recorded. Yet, after an unhappy event, Mary was always embarrassed and regretted that she had allowed herself to be out of control.

The deaths of Willie, Abraham and Tad dealt blows to Mary's heart and soul. Being so alone, she feared everything from thunder storms to strangers. Since her greatest fear was poverty, she carried her savings bonds in pockets in her petticoats to keep them safely with her at all times. This kind of eccentric behavior concerned Robert more and more, while his reassurances did little to dispel her worries. He conceived the idea of his mother living in a home where she would be free from worries and health cares. However, he knew she would never agree to live in a sanatarium voluntarily.

In Illinois, the only way to force his mother to live in such a home was through the courts. Robert, now a well-respected lawyer, had Mary brought to court and upon his tearful testimony, a jury found her insane. In the summer of 1875, she was sent to live at Bellevue Place in Batavia, Illinois. Here she felt like a prisoner although Robert visited and found her care excellent. For a little over three months Mary endured her surroundings while writing letters to friends on the outside asking for their help in freeing her. In August she wrote, "… I cannot understand why I should have been brought here."

Mary soon won her freedom and left the country as soon as possible. She lived quietly in the French countryside for several years until one day she fell and hurt her back. Crippled with pain and almost blind with cataracts, Mary weighed only 100 pounds. She returned home to live her final days in Springfield. Back once again in Elizabeth's home, she was lovingly cared for by the Hospital Sisters of St. Francis. When she died on July 16, 1882, she was not yet 64 years old.

BELLEVUE PLACE.

J   *Jealousy*

JEALOUSY FLARED UP in Mary Lincoln at times when she least expected it. Though Mary loved Abraham dearly, she was jealous of the long hours he spent away from her riding the Eighth Judicial Circuit. Then as President during the stressful years of the Civil War, duty called and they saw little of each other while living in the same house. Although Lincoln expressed his affection and concern for her in letters and telegrams, it never seemed to be enough for Mary.

When jealousy combined with ill health, Mary was known to throw a tantrum which embarrassed her husband as well as herself. One example of this took place at Malvern Hill, near the end of the war. This should have been a happy time for the couple, reviewing troops who were eagerly anticipating victory. To get there, Abraham rode ahead on horseback and Mary followed in an ambulance wagon with Mrs. Grant. But the roads were calf-deep in mud, the wagon was uncomfortable, and one terrific bump caused both women to hit their heads on the roof. It took them much longer than expected and Mary was beside herself.

When they finally arrived, Mary could see her husband on the field already parading in front of the troops with the attractive wife of General Ord. Mary was furious that her husband had not waited for her because SHE wanted to be the only one in the place of honor next to her husband! Some recalled that Mary became hysterical, calling Mrs. Ord vile names and insulting her loudly. Later, deeply humiliated, Mary returned to Washington to recover from the screaming migraine headache that could reduce her to such behavior.

Each time these explosions occurred, Abraham dealt with it in a loving, patient and kind manner. He understood that Mary's good character, her kindness and generosity far outweighed these tantrums. His love was strong enough to last through the bad times as well as the good.

K

Keckley

ELIZABETH KECKLEY AND Mary Todd Lincoln were unlikely best friends. Similar in age, they seemingly had nothing else in common. Elizabeth was born a slave while Mary was born into a well-to-do family which kept many slaves. While Mary's youth included pony rides and theater, Elizabeth worked in one household or another, praying never to be sold away from her dear mother.

Lizzie had a talent for sewing, and with this skill she eventually bought her freedom. Her ambition took her to Washington City where she was seamstress to many on Capitol Hill. When the new First Lady of the land arrived from far away Illinois, friends suggested that Mrs. Lincoln interview Mrs. Keckley for the job of her personal seamstress. It seemingly took only a few minutes for the two women to begin what would be a long-lasting friendship.

The lengthy fittings and hours of hand sewing on Mary's gowns offered plenty of time for heart-to-heart talks. Mary came to depend on Lizzie for her care, to travel with her and to visit soldiers in nearby hospitals. Lizzie's interest in helping poor, newly-freed slaves inspired Mary's support of the contraband effort at a time when it was unusual to do so.

Lizzie was a light skinned black woman who had only one son. He was so light that he passed for white and joined the Union army in the early days of the war. He was killed at the battle of Lexington, Missouri. When Willie died in the White House in 1862, Mary and Elizabeth had their bond strengthened by the similar loss of a beloved child.

Thus it was Lizzie whom Mary called for in the dark days after the assassination and it was Lizzie who traveled with Mary and Tad while neglecting her own sewing business. It was Lizzie whom Mary depended upon in New York City when she sought to sell some of her clothes to supplement her income.

But even this friendship was destined to end when Elizabeth decided to supplement her own lagging income (Mary was not paying her at this time) by publishing her memoirs entitled, *Behind the Scenes or Thirty Years a Slave and Four Years in the White House.* Mary felt betrayed that her friend would try to make money off their friendship and they parted ways. Elizabeth spent her last years in poverty in the National Home for Destitute Colored Women and Children which her contraband association had helped establish during the war.

L   *Lincoln*

TALL, TRUSTWORTHY AND honorable was Abraham Lincoln when he arrived in Springfield in 1837. He was already known to many in town as he had been a State Representative in the legislature which had been meeting in Vandalia. Since he had been helpful in getting the capital moved to Springfield, he had become friends with many of the important people in this new little prairie town. Quietly ambitious, his closest friends expected great things from him.

Arriving in April, Lincoln moved in with Joshua Speed above the little store on the square and did his best to begin to fulfill his ambitions. He was not one to sit idly by and watch others be successful; he too desired success. As a young man with limited resources, he had purchased property in the struggling town of New Salem and with friends to recommend and encourage him, he had become an influential legislator at a young age. Now in Springfield, he would build his legal career by running the law office he shared with John Todd Stuart, and by traveling the Eighth Judicial Circuit which opened up business, friendships and political contacts all at the same time.

Mary recognized Lincoln's desire to live a meaningful life and shared his hopes and dreams. Together they built a life based on love and respect. They both adored children and lovingly welcomed four sons into their family. They stood united when some extended family members chose to side with the South in the Civil War. Together, Abraham and Mary balanced the desire to save the Union with the need to rid the country of slavery. And together they faced the difficult years of sadness and death just as they had together embraced the joys of life.

$\mathcal{M}$ *Marriage*

THE MARRIAGE OF Abraham Lincoln and Mary Todd came after a rocky courtship. Since Mary's sister Elizabeth and her husband Ninian were against the union, it made sense to the couple to wed quickly before protests could be made. They did not tell of their plans until the day before the wedding and then things proceeded in a rush.

There was a quick trip to Chatterton's Jewelry Shop where a ring was chosen and engraved with the words "Love is Eternal." The minister needed to be arranged. Mary needed a dress. A few special friends needed to be invited. Reverend Dresser agreed to perform the wedding at his home that very evening but when Elizabeth and Ninian heard about it, they insisted that the ceremony be held in their parlor the following day. Elizabeth had little time to prepare. A receipt from the Bunn grocery store on that date indicates what was needed for the celebration that evening.

6# almonds	1.50
1 jar prunes	1.00
1 gal wine vinegar	.50
1 mackerel	.25
1 qt. sperm oil	<u>.50</u>
	$3.75

Obviously, there was not time to order the fancy pyramid of macaroons from Watson's Confectionary so admired by the socialites of Springfield, and the rumor spread that the wedding cake was still warm when served that evening. Mary chose to wear the same skirt and necklace that her sister Frances had worn at her wedding.

Then the candles were lit, the ceremony was held and Mary Todd became Mary Lincoln. She never looked back. She had chosen her husband and her life. The happy couple went straight to the Globe Tavern where they lived in the very same small room her sister Frances had lived in when she was first wed. The Lincolns would build themselves a marriage based on love and mutual respect. From their one little room, they had no where to go but up.

N

Names

Mary Ann Todd was her birth name until a younger sister was born and given the name Ann. Then it seemed to Mary that her middle name was no longer her very own so she immediately quit using it. Later, she was nicknamed Molly, a cute name for a delightful little girl who seemed to fit the name perfectly. It was used by family members into her adulthood and marriage. In fact, it is recorded that Abraham enjoyed calling her Molly in their courtship years.

Upon the birth of their first son, the endearing name of Molly was supplanted by the more matronly name **Mother**. In recollections and first person accounts, records indicate that Abraham referred to Mary as **Mother** throughout the rest of their lives. While Lincoln addressed his letters to "My dear wife" and Mary addressed her letters to "My dear husband", Victorian manners required that Mary call her husband Mr. Lincoln when speaking directly to him.

During their married life and in the years after the assassination, Mary made it very clear that her name was **Mary Lincoln**, omitting her maiden name Todd. Perhaps this was to impress upon people that her loyalty lay with her husband or perhaps it indicates her continued hurt feelings over the many Todd family members who never thought Mr. Lincoln quite good enough for them. However, even distancing herself from the Todd name didn't stop those who suspected her of having Southern sympathies. Had the public only known of her numerous hospital visits with injured soldiers, and her generosity to ex-slaves, they might have praised her instead of condemning her.

In a letter to Elizabeth Keckley in1867, Mary described some of this painful criticism.

> "Dear Lizzie,
> In this morning's *Tribune* there was a little article *evidently* designed to make capital *against* me just now- that three of my brothers were in the southern army during the war ... Why *harp* upon these *half* brothers, whom I never knew since they were infants, and scarcely then, for my early home was truly at a *boarding* school."

In her numerous letters, Mary signed herself Mary Lincoln or Mrs. A. Lincoln or Mrs. Lincoln, or with her initials M.L. She never signed letters with her Todd maiden name.

O Ocean Voyages

AS THE CIVIL War drew to a close, President Lincoln and Mary had only a short time to imagine a country at peace and an end to their sadness. They dreamed of riding a train all the way to California. They dreamed of sailing in a ship all the way to Europe. Maybe they would even see Jerusalem. It seemed that joy was awaiting them. And then the President was assassinated changing everything.

Mary did get to take two ocean voyages in her years of widowhood as she sought to find peace and happiness. Tad was with her on her first voyage in 1868. On October 1, they boarded the *City of Baltimore* steamer soon after Robert's wedding to Mary Harlan. Landing in Europe, Mary and Tad intended to stay only a few weeks in Frankfurt, Germany but ended up staying a couple of years. Here, Tad attended school and learned to speak English with a German accent. Here he grew to be a tall, handsome young man who resembled his father. Here he finally developed good manners, along with a suspicious cough. On their return voyage in 1871, Tad caught a cold which he just couldn't shake and to Mary's horror, it weakened him until he died in Chicago on July 15, 1871.

Mary took her second voyage in 1876 after a year of being considered "insane". When the courts declared her a fit person to control her property, she was free to travel and so she did-as far away from her only son Robert as possible. She headed to Pau, France where she hoped to restore her body and soul. Standing on a chair to hang a picture one day turned out to be a very bad thing to do. Mary fell and "broke her back" causing excruciating pain. It was time to return to Springfield and her loving big sister, Elizabeth.

On the voyage home, the ship lurched and Mary almost tumbled down a dangerous staircase. She was saved when a lady caught her big, black skirt and prevented disaster. The lady was a famous actress named Sarah Bernhardt who saw in Mary's eyes the yearning to join her husband in death. Later, Sarah reflected that she had "just done this unhappy woman the only service I ought not to have done her- I had saved her from death."

And so it was that an almost unrecognizable, white-haired Mary Lincoln came home for the last time. She was met at the docks by her great nephew, Edward Lewis Baker, Jr. who rode the train with her to Springfield. Needing a wheelchair now, Mary's traveling days were over.

$\mathcal{P}$ *Pension*

MARY'S FINANCIAL WOES worried her during the Presidential years and only grew worse after her husband's death. Spending money on clothes and jewelry always made Mary feel sophisticated until the bills came due. When the President died leaving no will, years went by and the estate was not settled. During this time, Mary's small family lived only on the little allowance allotted them. This was barely enough to live on, much less to repay her many debts. Fears were mounting with her IOU's when two years after the assassination, a desperate Mrs. Lincoln decided to take matters into her own hands and sell much of her clothing and jewelry to provide her family with some income.

Mary trusted two gentlemen to handle the sale in New York City. A private sale was one thing but putting her personal items on display in a Broadway storefront made Mary a laughing stock among people who were not sympathetic with her plight. It became ridiculed as ***The Old Clothes Scandal***. When the clothing and jewelry went unsold, Mary felt herself being deemed worthless as well. Eventually, almost all of her things were returned to her in huge trunks, but not before the embarrassing publicity thoroughly distressed her son Robert. Not long afterwards, Judge Davis, the executor, finalized the estate which provided the Lincoln family with about $80,000.

Many people felt that the country owed the President's widow nothing more, not even a yearly pension. Mary felt differently. Why, the widows of Civil War soldiers were paid pensions, so surely the widow of the Commander-in-Chief was owed one as well! Using her political know-how and writing letters to further her cause, Mary eventually succeeded in obtaining a pension of $3,000 per year.

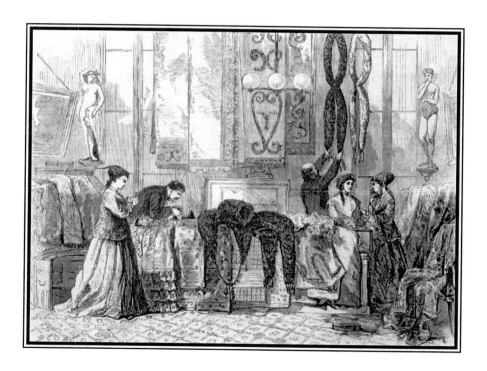

Q   *Quilt*

ELIZABETH KECKLEY, MARY'S dear friend during the White House years, became one of Mary's numerous ex-friends upon the publication of her memoir entitled, *Behind the Scenes or Thirty Years a Slave and Four Years in the White House.* While the book was kind to all the Lincolns, Mary felt betrayed by someone with whom she had shared her personal life and never spoke to Lizzie again.

Lizzie felt she had been fair and generous in her recollections of her days with the First Family and was hurt, sad and disappointed in Mary's response. Besides, she really needed the income from the book sales. As a sign of their long-standing friendship, Lizzie painstakingly pieced together a quilt made of Mary's many dress fabrics. She tried to give it to Mary as a peace offering, but was never given the chance for Lizzie had offended Robert as well as Mary and he rejected any attempts at contact between them.

Old and sad, Lizzie's life ended in seclusion with a photo of her dear friend, Mary Lincoln, hanging in her room.

$\mathcal{R}$ *Robert*

ROBERT LINCOLN WAS the firstborn of the Lincoln sons and the only one to live to adulthood. Robert was born while Abraham and Mary were still living in one room in the Globe Tavern, a rather noisy atmosphere for a new born baby.

Some of Robert's earliest memories would have been of a brother named Eddie who died before his fourth birthday, establishing a pattern of untimely deaths which Robert witnessed in his lifetime. A trip to Washington City with his newly-elected Congressman father introduced him to train travel and to his mother's wealthy family in Lexington whom they stopped to visit.

With his father riding the circuit for weeks on end, Robert felt little attachment to him and is described as being aloof from the rest of the Lincoln family. (In 1850, when Robert was seven, Lincoln rode the circuit 175 days.) At age 16, Robert expected to enroll straight into Harvard and was unpleasantly surprised to find that his Springfield education had been sorely lacking. A year in a preparatory school filled the gaps in his education and soon Harvard was the place he called home.

When Abraham Lincoln was asked to come east and give a speech at Cooper Union in New York, Robert was surprised by the positive reception his father received and the admiration of his friends at Harvard. Thus began Robert's respect for his father that grew during the difficult years of his presidency. When President Lincoln was assassinated, Robert was at his father's bedside as he breathed his last.

Never wanting to be known only as Abraham Lincoln's son, he sought to live his own life professionally and personally. Even so in death, he chose to be buried in Arlington Cemetery in Washington, DC rather than with his family in Springfield.

S *Spiritualism and Seances*

SPIRITUALISM IS THE belief that the spirits of the dead are so nearby that communication with them is possible. During the Civil War, it was a powerful way to deal with the tragic losses of thousands of young men in the prime of their lives. Loving wives and mothers could keep the departed one close through the belief that only a thin veil separated the living and the dead.

In her childhood, Mary probably encountered the spirit world through her Mammy Sally who tended to mix her Christian beliefs with traditional African beliefs in the visitation of the dead. During the War Between the States, Mary's best friend, Elizabeth Keckley, shared the desire to communicate with the dead after her own son was killed at the Battle of Wilson's Creek, Missouri in 1861. The two women visited mediums and believed they heard from their sons in the spirit world through gatherings called seances.

These seances were even held in the White House and the President was sometimes in attendance. However, he was skeptical and once proved a medium to be a fraud. Though Abraham Lincoln was not a believer in spiritualism, he did see visions and believed them to be true. More than once he saw a double vision of himself in his mirror, and he and Mary believed it meant that he would serve two terms as President, while the paler vision in the background indicated that he would die during his second term of office.

Mary found comfort in this fraudulent photo depicting Abraham watching over her from the next world, just a thin veil away.

T   *Tad and Willie*

TAD AND WILLIE, the "dear codgers" to their father, the "little angels" to their mother and the "troublemakers" to most everyone else, were a second Lincoln family after the death of Eddie. The cherished little boys were petted and coddled and allowed to do much as they pleased. Though Robert often felt that his younger brothers needed more discipline, Tad and Willie led the carefree life of small town America, free to roam the neighborhood with their many friends while always remembering to be home before dark.

Willie was known as the good boy who loved to read and go to church and planned on being a minister when he grew up. Tad, on the other hand, encouraged Willie to join in his many adventures and pranks. With his lisp, adults outside the family had difficulty understanding the boy, but Willie and their friends did just fine.

Then for one glorious year in the White House, Tad and Willie had the run of the place. When Willie died of typhoid fever in 1862, life changed markedly for Tad. He drew closer to his father as they comforted each other in their grief…and then unbelievably, his father was also gone. Tad realized then that he must go to school, learn to read and write and be a big boy. But first, he had to learn to dress himself!

Tad spent the following years being a comfort to his mother. They traveled to Europe together and Mary depended on Tad to be her mainstay when her life spiraled into sadness. Arriving home from their European tour, a mature, eighteen-year-old Tad was described by Mr. Jenkins at the Clifton house as "...a very lovable boy, quiet, gentle mannered and good natured, nothing loud or boisterous about him."

But Tad had developed a severe cold on the voyage home on top of the nagging cough which had plagued him in Europe. Medicine and loving care could not cure him and he died on July 15, 1871, leaving his mother desperately alone and heartbroken.

Willie Lincoln

$\mathcal{U}$ *Underwear*

THE UNDERWEAR WORN by ladies in the 1800's had three essential parts; a hoop skirt with petticoats, bloomers and a corset. It was a sign of maturity to wear fancy undergarments and Mary looked forward to the day when she would be old enough to wear such finery.

At nine years old, Mary Todd couldn't wait any longer. Her stepmother wouldn't allow her to have a hoop skirt yet, so she decided to make one instead. She convinced her cousin to join her adventure and they cut thin, pliable willow branches, forming them into a hoop contraption of sorts. But Mary's muslin dress was not big enough to easily flow over the awkward hoop causing not-so-elegant bulges. In her child's mind, however, she looked lovely and very grown up. On Sunday morning, Mary waltzed down the stairs feeling quite ladylike until she was humiliated by her stepmother's laughter and sent immediately back to her room to change into clothes more suitable for Sunday school. It was one of several small misadventures on her road to womanhood.

When grown up, Mary wore hoop skirts made of proper materials which included whalebone, purchased at John Williams and Company in Springfield. Atop the hoop skirt came layers of petticoats which helped conceal the ridges of the hoops. Under the hoop, a lady wore bloomers and pantaloons, made of comfortable cotton, trimmed in lace. Corsets were made of similar materials. The purpose of a corset was to accentuate a small waistline, so the garment was made with ties which were tightened by the hands of another person. Hence, wealthy women hired a maid to help them dress. In Mary's case, her seamstress Elizabeth Keckley filled both the roles of dressmaker and dressing attendant. Stockings completed the undergarments.

Crowded parties were made all the more crowded by the huge hoop skirts and many a hoop was dented, much as a car fender is dented nowadays.

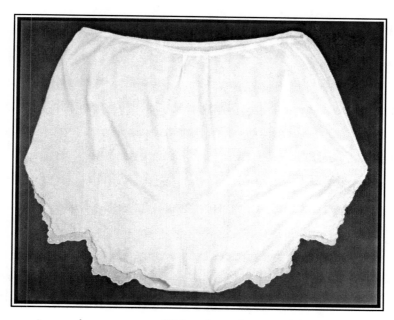

An undergarment of Mary's nicknamed bloomers.

$\mathcal{V}$ *Visiting*

AS THE CIVIL War progressed, thousands of injured soldiers were brought to makeshift hospitals in the Washington City area. Mary Lincoln visited them often bringing her special good cheer, flowers from the White House conservatory, and fruit from supplies meant for her family. She sat bedside by the hour writing letters for those who were unable. Since the Lincolns did not drink alcoholic beverages, any gifts of wine or whiskey were shared with the soldiers. Mary often made these visits alone or with Tad, and the public never knew of this generosity. However, one paper, the National Republican, became aware of her goodness and wrote this on January 26, 1863. "It may not be known that Mrs. Lincoln has contributed more than any lady in Washington, from her private purse, to alleviate the sufferings of our wounded soldiers."

Mary also became interested in the welfare of the ex-slaves who had been freed by Union troops. The number of these "contrabands" was staggering. From 400 in 1862, the number of refugees in the capital city rose to 40,000 newly freed men, women and children in 1865. The city was overwhelmed. Shelters were built using whatever materials were at hand be it planks, or barrels or mud. With her friend Elizabeth Keckley, Mary walked these sad back streets distributing food and blankets to the needy. Visiting these back alleys was certainly deemed controversial at the time but Mary was determined to be of help.

In a letter to her husband on November 3, 1862, Mary asked the President to "Please send check for $200…" for bed covering for the contrabands, which he did.

W *William H. Herndon*

WILLIAM HERNDON WAS Mr. Lincoln's law partner in Springfield. Abraham was fond of his junior partner and called him Billy, but Mary did not care for him. She was offended by his dependence on alcohol and never invited him to their home.

When President Lincoln was assassinated, people sought out William Herndon for information about the early life of their new hero. Mr. Herndon was not only glad to tell them everything he knew about Abraham, he decided to write a book about him. He visited with many of Lincoln's friends and relatives and took pages of notes.

The problem was that it was now thirty years later and memories were influenced by the way the questions were posed. Herndon also delivered speeches, to a country in post-Civil War turmoil ready to believe the worst about Mary Lincoln. When Herndon declared that Lincoln's parents had not been married, it made Abraham an illegitimate child. Robert immediately proved the marriage legitimate, but the damage was done. When Herndon said that Lincoln's only love was a young girl in New Salem who had died leaving him heartbroken, people believed that Abraham must never have

WILLIAM H. HERNDON WITH WHOM LINCOLN
WAS IN PARTNERSHIP 1844-1860.

loved Mary. Nuggets of truth were snuggled in between exaggerations and falsehoods. For obviously, Lincoln was sad over the death of Ann Rutledge but Herndon developed that sadness into a love affair that must be seen as questionable because Ann was engaged to someone else. Lincoln's keen sense of honor would never have allowed him to court a betrothed woman. Yet, the more Mary decried his claims, the more he was believed. Such is the nature of publicity.

In December 1873, Herndon gave a speech in Springfield in which he insisted that Lincoln was not a Christian. Mary's reaction to this latest allegation was to become even more fearful, sleepless and dependent on drugs to calm her nerves.

The public never knew that Herndon himself was a sick, unkempt man whose law practice had shrunk to nearly nothing. He was living 6 miles north of Springfield, a long, wearying walk for a heavy drinker. He did not live to see the publication of the book which was to be the crowning achievement of his life.

X eXecutive mansion

THE LINCOLN FAMILY moved into the eXecutive mansion when Abraham was sworn in as President in 1861. What a difference from their little house on 8th Street! The East Room alone was the size of their old home!

The White House had been rebuilt in 1814 after the British burned it in the War of 1812 but by the time the Lincolns moved in, the house had been utterly neglected and worn out. There were rats in the basement, wallpaper was peeling, draperies had holes and it looked like an "old and unsuccessful hotel" to Mary's secretary, William Stoddard.

Mary took one tour of the White House and knew exactly what needed to be done. First, she saw to it that the house was cleaned from top to bottom. New furnaces were installed as well as gas and water lines. Then, she headed to New York City to spend the $20,000 allocated to her for furnishings. With Mary's good taste and high standards, it was easy to overspend the allowance on furniture, velvet carpet, silk draperies and fine china.

When the bills came due, Mary lived in fear that her husband would be upset at the amount she had spent. She was right; her husband was furious that so much money had been spent on "flub dubs", as he called them. But the house looked better than it had in years. During State dinners, receptions and levees, the house sparkled and guests were impressed.

Needing to pay the bills that kept coming, Mary came up with ingenious ideas to make money. She cut corners and lived frugally until the next shopping trip tempted her to buy more. Money issues plagued her the rest of her years as the President's wife and afterward, as his widow.

Y Youth

MARY TODD WAS born on December 13, 1818 in the Todd home on Short Street, just steps from her Grandmother Parker's home. This pleasant situation allowed the grandchildren easy access to the love and care of their grandmother while their mother was busy caring for new babies who needed her attention. Elizabeth was the eldest child; then came Frances, Levi, Mary, Robert, Ann and George. This was the house which Mary called home, although soon after her mother died and her father remarried, the family moved to a larger house on Main Street.

This was horse country and when a band of strolling players was stranded in Lexington, Mary's father bought her one of their dancing ponies. In a story handed down in the Todd family to her niece Katherine Helm, Mary supposedly galloped the mile down the road to Henry Clay's home to show him her new horse flesh. Mr. Clay, the famous politician, was entertaining important gentlemen that day, but Mary, flushed and mussed from the ride, insisted that "Mary Todd wished to see him."

When he came out, his guests delighted in watching this charming, vivacious girl whip the pony into a two-legged dance, after which Mary joined the men for dinner. Never one to be intimidated, Mary eagerly took part in the adult conversation and when the discussion turned toward Mr. Clay's presidential possibilities, Mary expressed her desire to one day live in the White House as well. "Well," laughed Mr. Clay, "if I am ever President I shall expect Mary Todd to be one of my first guests. Will you come?" Mary accepted with enthusiasm. "If you were not already married," she said, graciously, "I would wait for you."

Grandmother Parker's home in Lexington, Kentucky.

Z   *Mrs. Lincoln's Zouaves*

WITH SOLDIERS IN the White House, soldiers on the lawn and soldiers marching through the streets of Washington City, it is not surprising that the sons of the President should choose playing soldier as their favorite game. Mrs. Lincoln obliged and made Zouave uniforms for her sons and their soldier dolls as well. These bright red and blue uniforms made their play more fun.

Joining with them were their friends from around the corner, Bud and Holly Taft. Together with the Lincoln boys they called themselves Mrs. Lincoln's Zouaves and defended the White House from rebel invaders. With the run of the house, they could practice marching inside or out, with little regard for the noise and chaos they sometimes caused. Their favorite place to defend the mansion was on the roof. This was at times their fort and at others, a deck of a ship. A small log pointing south was their cannon, like the Quaker cannons which the real armies used to fool each other into thinking they had superior forces for their defense.

Up and down the stairs, to the roof, and out to the garden ran Mrs. Lincoln's Zouaves. Willie was the colonel, Bud Taft the Major, Holly Taft was the Captain and Tad was the drum major. When the doll, Jack, fell asleep on guard duty, Tad interrupted a cabinet meeting seeking a pardon so the doll would not have to be hanged. To the irritation of his cabinet, President Lincoln smiled and dutifully wrote:

The doll Jack is pardoned, by order of the President. A. Lincoln.

TAD LINCOLN IN HIS ZOUAVE UNIFORM

Printed in the United States
116522LV00002B/259-1098/P

9 781434 368270